refocus

viewing problems from God's perspective

©2011 by Because of Jesus Publishing
P.O. Box 3064
Broken Arrow, OK 74013
ISBN : 0-9779972-8-6
Printed in the USA

Cover design and layout: Shannan Orr

Author's note: The Message is a modern translation written to capture the conversational feel of the original language in contemporary English.

Author's note: The Amplified Bible expands the meaning of words in the text by placing synonyms and definitions in parentheses and brackets to give the reader a more complete grasp of meaning of the words as they were understood in the original languages.

A crisis is any time I look to my own abilities instead of trusting God's ability. This book was born during one of those times in my own life. I still pick it up whenever I am tempted to view my circumstances through my own limitations and failures.

I pray that as you take a few minutes to flip through these pages, God will use them to help you refocus on His great, unconditional love for you. His voice of Truth is speaking words of life, peace, and hope today in contradiction to the lies that are common to us all.

-Shannan

refocus

–Part 1–

Why refocus?

Everyone wants to be free from the anxiety, depression, confusion, addictions, and pain that are common in life.

But where does freedom come from?

"... you will know the Truth, and
the Truth will set you free."

John 8:32 AMP

God is Truth. Everything He says is true, because it's who He is.

Jesus answered, "I am the way and the truth and the life."

John 14:6 NIV

In the beginning, God said everything was good and that people were **very** *good–like Him, made in His image.*

God looked over everything
he had made; it was so good,
so very good!

Genesis 1:31 MSG

And it was true, because Truth said so.

… it is impossible for God to lie…

Hebrews 6:18 NIV

Shortly after God created mankind in His image, they were presented with a lie; a version of the same lie that still comes to every person,

"You would be better off trusting your own perspective rather than what God says."

The serpent told the Woman, "You won't die. God knows that the moment you eat from that tree, you'll see what's really going on."

Genesis 3:4-5 MSG

They didn't choose evil because they wanted to be evil. Their decision was based on their desire for something good. Adam & Eve wanted to be like God.

"... you will be like God, knowing the difference between good and evil and blessing and calamity.

Genesis 3:5 AMP

The problem started when, instead of believing what Truth had told them–that they were ***already like God****–the ancestors of all mankind focused on their own viewpoint.*

They became convinced that they could get what they wanted in their own way.

The woman was convinced. She saw that the tree was beautiful and its fruit looked delicious, and she wanted the wisdom it would give her.

Genesis 3:6 NLT

They reasoned away Truth's decree and made what they considered a "good" choice based on their flawed perception.

So she took some of the fruit and ate it. Then she gave some to her husband, who was with her, and he ate it, too.

Genesis 3:6 NLT

In the same way that Adam and Eve's focus led to destruction, my choices– based on my own distorted opinion apart from God–can take me to places of pain, fear, and turmoil.

There is a way which seems right to a man and appears straight before him, but at the end of it is the way of death.

Proverbs 14:12 AMP

My belief system affects all of my decisions and, ultimately, all of my actions.

A good man brings good things out of the good stored up in his heart, and an evil man brings evil things out of the evil stored up in his heart.

Luke 6:45 NIV

When my actions–based upon my beliefs–conflict with others who have their own twisted opinion of truth, trouble multiplies.

Where do you think all these appalling wars and quarrels come from? Do you think they just happen? Think again. They come about because you want your own way, and fight for it deep inside yourselves.

James 4:1 MSG

Jesus warned me that I would have trouble in this world, but in the same instant He said I could have perfect peace and confidence by focusing on what He has already done for me.

"I have told you these things, so that in Me you may have [perfect] peace and confidence. In the world you have tribulation and trials and distress and frustration; but be of good cheer [take courage; be confident, certain, undaunted]! For I have overcome the world. [I have deprived it of power to harm you and have conquered it for you.]"

John 16:33 AMP

If I want my life to be different, I can't keep viewing my world through this faulty lens of human perception.

Don't copy the behavior and customs of this world, but let God transform you into a new person by changing the way you think. Then you will learn to know God's will for you, which is good and pleasing and perfect.

Romans 12:2 NIV

When my focus is on God's love for me and what Truth says about me, my decisions and actions will agree with His opinion, and I can live the life He wants for me.

But what happens when we live God's way? He brings gifts into our lives, much the same way that fruit appears in an orchard things like affection for others, exuberance about life, serenity. We develop a willingness to stick with things, a sense of compassion in the heart, and a conviction that a basic holiness permeates things and people. We find ourselves involved in loyal commitments, not needing to force our way in life, able to marshal and direct our energies wisely.

Galatians 5:22-23 MSG

This is how Jesus lived His life on earth. When He encountered difficult people and circumstances, He focused on His Father's good opinion of Him.

"You are my Son, whom I love;
with you I am well pleased."

Luke 3:22 NIV

Making choices apart from what God says about me only brings more pain into my life.

It is obvious what kind of life develops out of trying to get your own way all the time: repetitive, loveless, cheap sex; a stinking accumulation of mental and emotional garbage; frenzied and joyless grabs for happiness; trinket gods; magic-show religion; paranoid loneliness; cutthroat competition; all-consuming-yet-never-satisfied wants; a brutal temper; an impotence to love or be loved; divided homes and divided lives; small-minded and lopsided pursuits; the vicious habit of depersonalizing everyone into a rival; uncontrolled and uncontrollable addictions; ugly parodies of community.
I could go on.

Galatians 5:19-21 MSG

I don't want that kind of life.
It's the not kind of life that
Jesus came to give me.

"I came so they can have real and
eternal life, more and better life
than they ever dreamed of."

John 10:10 MSG

This situation is only a crisis if I decide I'm smarter than God and reject what He says about it.

So do not throw away this confident trust in the Lord. Remember the great reward it brings you!

Hebrews 10:35 NLT

I do not want to take another bite from the fruit of my own judgment and start this cycle of pain again. When the opportunity arises to see things either from my perspective or from God's, I want to surrender my way of thinking and refocus to His viewpoint.

"Today I have given you the choice between life and death, between blessings and curses. Now I call on heaven and earth to witness the choice you make. Oh, that you would choose life, so that you and your descendants might live!"

Deuteronomy 30:19 NLT

Jesus, You called Yourself the Truth. Reveal Yourself to me. Help me recognize the lies that bring pain into my life. Help me to accept that what You say about me is true. I want to refocus.

"Here's what I want you to do: Find a quiet, secluded place so you won't be tempted to role-play before God. Just be there as simply and honestly as you can manage. The focus will shift from you to God, and you will begin to sense his grace."

Matthew 6:6 MSG

You created me; You created the universe. Surely You have a better perspective than I do.

Trust God from the bottom of your heart; don't try to figure out everything on your own. Listen for God's voice in everything you do, everywhere you go; he's the one who will keep you on track. Don't assume that you know it all.
Run to God! Run from evil! Your body will glow with health, your very bones will vibrate with life!

Proverbs 3:5-8 MSG

I want to trust You and reject any voice that speaks anything other than what You say.

"... he walks on before them, and the sheep follow him because they know his voice. They will never [on any account] follow a stranger, but will run away from him because they do not know the voice of strangers or recognize their call."

John 10: 4-5 AMP

I surrender my limited, human viewpoint to the Spirit of the living God, who is the Truth.

…you have received the Holy Spirit, and he lives within you, so you don't need anyone to teach you what is true. For the Spirit teaches you everything you need to know, and what he teaches is true—it is not a lie. So just as he has taught you, remain in fellowship with Christ.

1 John 2:27 NLT

refocus

–Part 2–

Surrendering my opinion; refocusing on Truth

I see this lie has brought me pain...

This won't work. I just don't have what it takes to trust God.

Help me to see You, Truth...

[Not in your own strength] for it is God Who is all the while effectually at work in you [energizing and creating in you the power and desire], both to will and to work for His good pleasure and satisfaction and delight.

Philippians 2:13 AMP

refocus

I see this lie has brought me pain...

God won't help me—He's too angry with me.

Help me to see You, Truth...

"To me this is like the days of Noah, when I swore that the waters of Noah would never again cover the earth. So now I have sworn not to be angry with you, never to rebuke you again. Though the mountains be shaken and the hills be removed, yet my unfailing love for you will not be shaken nor my covenant of peace be removed," says the LORD, who has compassion on you.

Isaiah 54:9-10 NIV

refocus

I see this lie has brought me pain...

God must not love me. If He really loved me, I would not have all this trouble.

Help me to see You, Truth...

Does it mean he no longer loves us if we have trouble or calamity, or are persecuted, or hungry, or destitute, or in danger, or threatened with death?... No, despite all these things, overwhelming victory is ours through Christ, who loved us. And I am convinced that nothing can ever separate us from God's love.

Romans 8:35, 37-38 NLT

refocus

I see this lie has brought me pain...

God must not love me. If He really loved me, He would do things the way I think they should be done.

Help me to see You, Truth...

I know what I'm doing. I have it all planned out—plans to take care of you, not abandon you, plans to give you the future you hope for.

Jeremiah 29:11 MSG

refocus

*I see this lie
has brought me pain...*

God could never love me.
I'm too bad.

Help me to see You, Truth...

Do you think anyone is going to be able to drive a wedge between us and Christ's love for us? There is no way! Not trouble, not hard times, not hatred, not hunger, not homelessness, not bullying threats, not backstabbing, not even the worst sins listed in Scripture.

Romans 8:35 MSG

refocus

I see this lie
has brought me pain...

God can't forgive me.
I've done too many wrong things.

Help me to see You, Truth...

... God made you alive with Christ, for he forgave all our sins. He canceled the record of the charges against us and took it away by nailing it to the cross.

Colossians 2:13-14 NLT

refocus

I see this lie
has brought me pain...

I'm too messed up to ever be right with God.

Help me to see You, Truth...

We know very well that we are not set right with God by rule-keeping but only through personal faith in Jesus Christ. How do we know? We tried it—and we had the best system of rules the world has ever seen! Convinced that no human being can please God by self-improvement, we believed in Jesus as the Messiah so that we might be set right before God by trusting in the Messiah, not by trying to be good.

Galatians 2:15-16 MSG

refocus

I see this lie
has brought me pain...

I should be ashamed of all of the wrong choices I have made.

Help me to see You, Truth...

Now there is no condemnation for those who belong to Christ Jesus.

Romans 8:1-2 NLT

refocus

I see this lie
has brought me pain...

There must be something
wrong with me.

Help me to see You, Truth...

Yet now he has reconciled you to himself through the death of Christ in his physical body. As a result, he has brought you into his own presence, and you are holy and blameless as you stand before him without a single fault.

Colossians 1:22 NLT

refocus

I see this lie
has brought me pain...

I deserve this trouble in my life; God must be punishing me.

Help me to see You, Truth...

Because of the sacrifice of the Messiah, his blood poured out on the altar of the Cross, we're a free people—free of penalties and punishments chalked up by all our misdeeds.
And not just barely free, either. Abundantly free!

Ephesians 1:7 MSG

refocus

I see this lie
has brought me pain...

I have made too many mistakes. I will have to pay for them forever.

Help me to see You, Truth...

Yet God, with undeserved kindness, declares that we are righteous. He did this through Christ Jesus when he freed us from the penalty for our sins.

Romans 3:24 NLT

refocus

I see this lie
has brought me pain...

This problem is my fault.
I have to figure it out myself.

Help me to see You, Truth...

Instead of trusting in our own strength or wits to get out of it, we were forced to trust God totally—not a bad idea since he's the God who raises the dead! And he did it, rescued us from certain doom. And he'll do it again, rescuing us as many times as we need rescuing.

2 Corinthians 1:9-10 MSG

refocus

I see this lie has brought me pain...

I don't have what I need.
I have to get it myself.

Help me to see You, Truth...

What shall we say about such wonderful things as these? If God is for us, who can ever be against us? Since he did not spare even his own Son but gave him up for us all, won't he also give us everything else?

Romans 8:31-32 NLT

refocus

I see this lie
has brought me pain...

I need what I want, and I need it now.

Help me to see You, Truth...

...let endurance and steadfastness and patience have full play and do a thorough work, so that you may be [people] perfectly and fully developed [with no defects], lacking in nothing.

James 1:4 AMP

refocus

I see this lie has brought me pain...

I'm too afraid of God to talk to Him about this.

Help me to see You, Truth...

This High Priest of ours understands our weaknesses, for he faced all of the same testings we do, yet he did not sin. So let us come boldly to the throne of our gracious God. There we will receive his mercy, and we will find grace to help us when we need it most.

Hebrews 4:15-16 NLT

refocus

I see this lie
has brought me pain...

My situation is too horrible;
nothing good can come from it.

Help me to see You, Truth...

He knows us far better than we know ourselves... and keeps us present before God. That's why we can be so sure that every detail in our lives of love for God is worked into something good.

Romans 8:27-28 MSG

refocus

I see this lie
has brought me pain...

I can't do it.
My problem is too hard.

Help me to see You, Truth...

"I am the LORD, the God of all mankind.
Is anything too hard for me?"

Jeremiah 32:27 NIV

refocus

I see this lie
has brought me pain...

I can't do it.
I am inadequate.

Help me to see You, Truth...

Now may the God of peace [Who is the Author and the Giver of peace]... strengthen (complete, perfect) and make you what you ought to be and equip you with everything good that you may carry out His will; [while He Himself] works in you and accomplishes that which is pleasing in His sight, through Jesus Christ.

Hebrews 13:20-21 AMP

refocus

I see this lie
has brought me pain...

This sin is too big.

Help me to see You, Truth...

...where sin increased and abounded, grace (God's unmerited favor) has surpassed it and increased the more and superabounded.

Romans 5:20 AMP

refocus

I see this lie
has brought me pain...

I'm so confused; I don't know what to do.

Help me to see You, Truth...

If you don't know what you're doing, pray to the Father. He loves to help. You'll get his help, and won't be condescended to when you ask for it. Ask boldly, believingly, without a second thought.

James 1:5-6 MSG

refocus

I see this lie
has brought me pain...

I feel so powerless in this situation.

Help me to see You, Truth...

"... My grace is all you need. My power works best in weakness..."

2 Corinthians 12:9 NLT

refocus

I see this lie
has brought me pain...

I don't know how to change myself.

Help me to see You, Truth...

Those who think they can do it on their own end up obsessed with measuring their own moral muscle but never get around to exercising it in real life. Those who trust God's action in them find that God's Spirit is in them—living and breathing God! Focusing on the self is the opposite of focusing on God.

Romans 8:5, 7 MSG

refocus

I see this lie
has brought me pain...

I have no purpose.

Help me to see You, Truth...

It's in Christ that we find out who we are and what we are living for. Long before we first heard of Christ and got our hopes up, he had his eye on us, had designs on us for glorious living, part of the overall purpose he is working out in everything and everyone.

Ephesians 1:11-12 MSG

refocus

I see this lie
has brought me pain...

My life is not worth living.

Help me to see You, Truth...

My old self has been crucified with Christ. It is no longer I who live, but Christ lives in me. So I live in this earthly body by trusting in the Son of God, who loved me and gave himself for me.

Galatians 2:20 NLT

I see this lie
has brought me pain...

No one wants me.

Help me to see You, Truth...

Even before he made the world, God loved us and chose us in Christ to be holy and without fault in his eyes. God decided in advance to adopt us into his own family by bringing us to himself through Jesus Christ. This is what he wanted to do, and it gave him great pleasure.

Ephesians 1:4-5 NLT

I see this lie
has brought me pain...

No one will ever love me.

Help me to see You, Truth...

But God shows and clearly proves His [own] love for us by the fact that while we were still sinners, Christ (the Messiah, the Anointed One) died for us.

Romans 5:8 AMP

refocus

I see this lie
has brought me pain...

I'm worthless.

Help me to see You, Truth...

... God paid a ransom to save you from the empty life you inherited from your ancestors. And the ransom he paid was not mere gold or silver. It was the precious blood of Christ, the sinless, spotless Lamb of God.

1 Peter 1:18-19 NLT

I see this lie
has brought me pain...

I'm so alone.

Help me to see You, Truth...

...for He [God] Himself has said, I will not in any way fail you nor give you up nor leave you without support. [I will] not, [I will] not, [I will] not in any degree leave you helpless nor forsake nor let [you] down (relax My hold on you)! [Assuredly not!]

Hebrews 13:5 AMP

refocus

I see this lie
has brought me pain...

No one cares about me.

Help me to see You, Truth...

"What's the price of two or three pet canaries? Some loose change, right? But God never overlooks a single one. And he pays even greater attention to you, down to the last detail—even numbering the hairs on your head! So don't be intimidated by all this bully talk. You're worth more than a million canaries."

Luke 12:6-7 MSG

refocus

I see this lie has brought me pain...

God doesn't care about my problems.

Help me to see You, Truth...

Casting the whole of your care [all your anxieties, all your worries, all your concerns, once and for all] on Him, for He cares for you affectionately and cares about you watchfully.

1 Peter 5:7 AMP

refocus

I see this lie
has brought me pain...

I'm overwhelmed and worried.

Help me to see You, Truth...

Instead of worrying, pray.
Let petitions and praises shape your worries into prayers, letting God know your concerns. Before you know it, a sense of God's wholeness, everything coming together for good, will come and settle you down. It's wonderful what happens when Christ displaces worry at the center of your life.

Philippians 4:6 MSG

refocus

I see this lie
has brought me pain...

I'll never have peace.

Help me to see You, Truth...

"I am leaving you with a gift—
peace of mind and heart. And the peace I give is a gift the world cannot give. So don't be troubled or afraid."

John 14:27 NLT

refocus

Shannan Orr's life was radically transformed when she began to let go of her self-focus and accept what God says about her is true. Her desire is to help people of all ages experience the same life-changing truths that have brought life to her own soul. A children's minister for more than 30 years, she is co-author of the "Yes, I Am" curriculum, which teaches young hearts how much God loves them, and who they are because of Jesus.

If God has used "Refocus" to speak to your heart, Shannan would love to hear from you.

Email: Shannan@RefocusOnTruth.com

Website: RefocusOnTruth.com

Because of Jesus Ministries
Attn: Shannan Orr
P.O.Box 3064
Broken Arrow, OK 74013